EXPLORING THE STATES

Arkansas

THE NATURAL STATE

by Emily Rose Oachs

BELLWETHER MEDIA • MINNEAPOLIS, MN

Note to Librarians, Teachers, and Parents:

Blastoff! Readers are carefully developed by literacy experts and combine standards-based content with developmentally appropriate text.

Level 1 provides the most support through repetition of high-frequency words, light text, predictable sentence patterns, and strong visual support.

Level 2 offers early readers a bit more challenge through varied simple sentences, increased text load, and less repetition of high-frequency words.

Level 3 advances early-fluent readers toward fluency through increased text and concept load, less reliance on visuals, longer sentences, and more literary language.

Level 4 builds reading stamina by providing more text per page, increased use of punctuation, greater variation in sentence patterns, and increasingly challenging vocabulary.

Level 5 encourages children to move from "learning to read" to "reading to learn" by providing even more text, varied writing styles, and less familiar topics.

Whichever book is right for your reader, Blastoff! Readers are the perfect books to build confidence and encourage a love of reading that will last a lifetime!

This edition first published in 2014 by Bellwether Media, Inc.

No part of this publication may be reproduced in whole or in part without written permission of the publisher. For information regarding permission, write to Bellwether Media, Inc., Attention: Permissions Department, 5357 Penn Avenue South, Minneapolis, MN 55419.

Library of Congress Cataloging-in-Publication Data

Oachs, Emily Rose.
 Arkansas / by Emily Rose Oachs.
   pages cm. – (Blastoff! readers. Exploring the states)
 Includes bibliographical references and index.
 Summary: "Developed by literacy experts for students in grades three through seven, this book introduces young readers to the geography and culture of Arkansas"–Provided by publisher.
 ISBN 978-1-62617-003-2 (hardcover : alk. paper)
 1. Arkansas–Juvenile literature. I. Title.
 F411.3.O34 2014
 976.7–dc23
                                                                                    2013002380

Printed in the United States of America, North Mankato, MN.

Table of Contents

Where Is Arkansas?

Arkansas covers 53,179 square miles (137,733 square kilometers) in the southern United States. The Mississippi River forms the state's eastern border. It separates Arkansas from Tennessee and Mississippi. Missouri lies north of Arkansas. To the south is Louisiana. Texas and Oklahoma are neighbors to the west.

The Arkansas River cuts the state in half. The river flows from west to east, where it joins the Mississippi River. Little Rock, the state capital, is in central Arkansas. It was built on the banks of the Arkansas River.

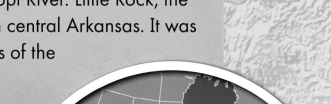

Oklahoma

Missouri

Tennessee

Mammoth
Spring

● Springdale
● Fayetteville

Arkansas

Arkansas River

Fort Smith

★ Little Rock

● Hot Springs
National Park

Mississippi River

Mississippi

Texas   Louisiana

History

Native Americans lived in Arkansas thousands of years ago. The French were the first Europeans to permanently settle the area. In 1803, the United States bought Arkansas as part of the **Louisiana Purchase**. Arkansas became a state on June 15, 1836. In 1861, it joined the **Confederacy** with other southern states. They fought the **Civil War** against the northern **Union** states.

Civil War

Arkansas Timeline!

1541: Spanish explorer Hernando de Soto is the first European to set foot in Arkansas.

1686: Frenchman Henri de Tonty sets up Arkansas Post. It is the first permanent European settlement in the area.

1803: France sells land to the United States in the Louisiana Purchase.

1830s: The government forces Arkansas' Native Americans west into Indian Territory.

1836: Arkansas becomes the twenty-fifth state.

1861: Arkansas joins the Confederacy.

1861-1865: The Civil War is fought between the northern and southern states.

1868: Arkansas rejoins the Union.

1957: Nine African-American students attend Little Rock's Central High School. Before them, the school was for whites only.

1992: William J. Clinton, an Arkansas native, is elected the forty-second President of the United States.

Hernando de Soto

Little Rock Nine

William J. Clinton

The Land

Ozark Mountains

Arkansas' Climate
average °F

spring
Low: 52°
High: 72°

summer
Low: 70°
High: 90°

fall
Low: 53°
High: 73°

winter
Low: 34°
High: 52°

Did you know?
Arkansas has mild winters and hot summers. The mountains have cooler weather than the rest of the state.

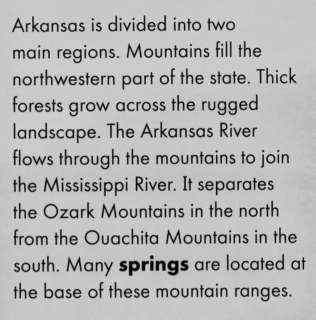

Arkansas is divided into two main regions. Mountains fill the northwestern part of the state. Thick forests grow across the rugged landscape. The Arkansas River flows through the mountains to join the Mississippi River. It separates the Ozark Mountains in the north from the Ouachita Mountains in the south. Many **springs** are located at the base of these mountain ranges.

Plains cover southeastern Arkansas. The Mississippi **Delta** surrounds the Mississippi River in the eastern third of the state. Many farmers grow crops in the rich soil here. The western **Gulf** Coastal Plain is home to forests and **bayous**. Its rolling landscape stretches through the southern part of the state.

Springs

Spring water can be hot or cold. The deeper underground the water goes, the warmer it is when it reaches the surface. Many springs in Arkansas produce pure water. Others are rich in **minerals**. Mammoth Spring in the Ozarks is the state's largest spring. About 10 million gallons (38 million liters) of chilly water gush from the spring each hour.

Arkansas is famous for its hot springs. Mineral water flows from 47 springs at Hot Springs National Park in the Ouachitas. The water's temperature is around 143 degrees Fahrenheit (62 degrees Celsius). Some people believe these waters have healing powers. **Tourists** come from all over to bathe in Arkansas' springs.

Mammoth Spring

Did you know?
NASA used to place moon rocks in spring water from Hot Springs National Park. The pure water kept the rocks bacteria-free while NASA studied them for signs of life!

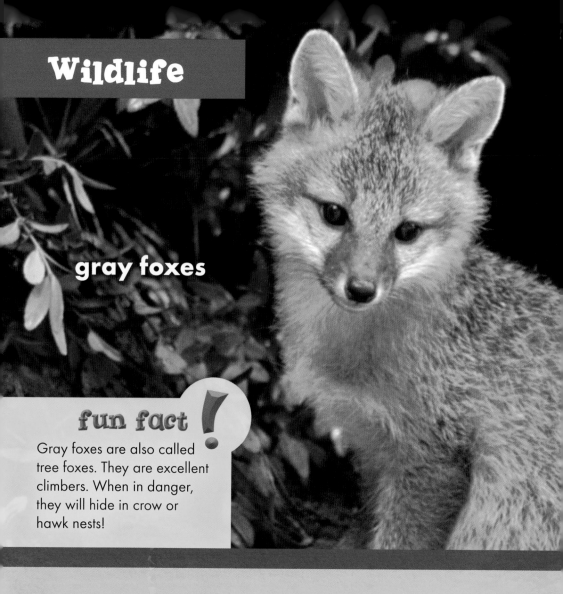

gray foxes

fun fact !

Gray foxes are also called tree foxes. They are excellent climbers. When in danger, they will hide in crow or hawk nests!

About half of Arkansas is forests. Many animals take shelter in these woods. Gray foxes live in their thick cover. In the Ozarks, black bears search for berries and nuts. Bobcats wander the hills and forests. Deer, opossums, and rabbits roam the lowlands. In southern Arkansas, armadillos are a common sight. Wild hogs known as razorbacks make their homes throughout the state.

Did you know?
Mockingbirds can copy up to 200 sounds. They can sound like a cat meowing or even a car alarm!

mockingbird

wild hog

black bear

The Mississippi Flyway passes through Arkansas. This **migration** route trails the Mississippi River. Geese, ducks, and hummingbirds follow it through Arkansas twice a year. Mockingbirds live all over Arkansas. Blue jays, cardinals, and barn owls roost along the edges of the forests. Hawks and bald eagles glide overhead in search of prey.

Landmarks

Arkansas holds a wide variety of attractions. Crater of Diamonds State Park is the only active diamond mine in the United States. The park allows tourists to dig for diamonds and keep whatever gems they find. The Blanchard Springs Caverns are a stunning underground world in the Ozark National Forest. Tours bring visitors through the caves' magnificent rock formations.

The Crystal Bridges Museum of American Art is in Bentonville. It is filled with beautiful artwork from throughout the nation's history. The William J. Clinton Presidential Center stands near the river in Little Rock. The center honors the forty-second President of the United States, who was born and raised in Arkansas.

fun fact

At dusk, visitors at the Blanchard Springs Caverns can watch a giant colony of bats exit the cave to feed.

Blanchard Springs Caverns

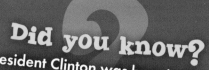

Did you know?

President Clinton was born in Hope, Arkansas. He and his family later moved to Hot Springs.

William J. Clinton Presidential Center

Little Rock

French explorers founded Little Rock in 1820. The capital city stands on a cliff beside the Arkansas River. Home to around 193,500 people, it is the state's largest city.

In 1957, an important historical event took place in Little Rock. Before the 1950s, African-American and white students were not allowed to attend the same schools. In 1954, the U.S. government said schools needed to **integrate**. The Governor of Arkansas disagreed. In 1957, he sent soldiers to stop nine African-American students from entering Little Rock's Central High School. A crowd of white people also screamed at the students. President Eisenhower had to send 1,000 troops to help the students enter the school safely.

Little Rock Nine

fun fact

The nine students were awarded the Congressional Gold Medal in 1999. This is one of the most important awards the U.S. government can give.

fun fact

The headquarters of the superstore Walmart is located in Bentonville. Sam Walton opened the first Walmart store in 1962.

Many Arkansans have **service jobs**. They work in hospitals, hotels, and restaurants. Some also work for the government. People who work in tourism provide services to around 20 million visitors each year.

About two-fifths of Arkansas is farmland. Farmers raise chickens, pigs, and cattle. They also grow cotton, corn, wheat, and soybeans. Arkansas produces more rice than any other state. At factories, workers build car and airplane parts. Others make chicken products. Some Arkansans dig for minerals throughout the state. Coal and natural gas are found in the Arkansas Valley. Workers drill for oil in the south.

Where People Work in Arkansas

manufacturing
12%

services
69%

farming and
natural resources
5%

government
14%

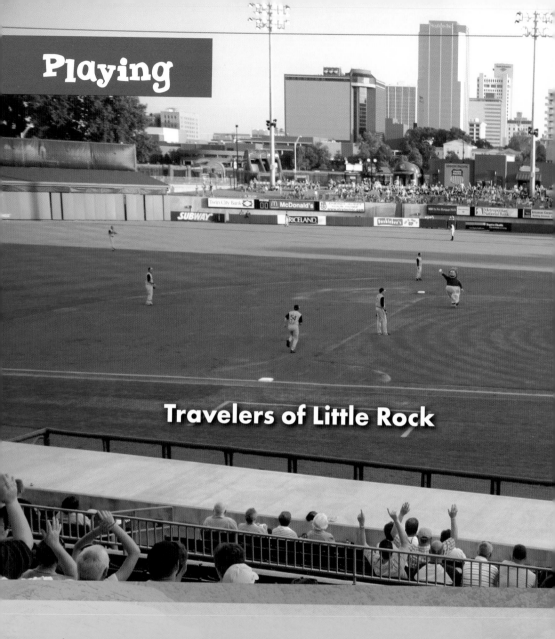

Playing

Travelers of Little Rock

Arkansas offers many outdoor activities. People hike in the Ozarks and Ouachitas. The rivers and streams are great for fishing or canoeing. Visitors can go boating or waterskiing on one of the state's many lakes.

The Arkansas Travelers of Little Rock are a favorite minor league baseball team. They have entertained sports fans since 1901. Car racing is another popular sport. The Batesville Speedway is a dirt track that draws crowds from all over the state. Arkansans also love **rodeos**. These events feature calf roping, bull riding, and barrel racing.

Collard Greens

Ingredients:

1 bunch collard greens, rinsed, trimmed, and chopped

1 medium onion, chopped

2 smoked ham hocks

2 (10.5-ounce) cans condensed chicken broth

21 fluid ounces water (equal to 2 broth cans)

1 tablespoon distilled white vinegar

Salt and pepper to taste

Directions:

1. Place the collard greens, ham hocks, and onions in a large pot.

2. Mix in the chicken broth, water, and vinegar.

3. Season with salt and pepper.

4. Bring to a boil, then reduce heat to low.

5. Simmer 1 hour.

New Year's meal

Did you know?
On New Year's Day, many Arkansans eat collard greens, cornbread, and black-eyed peas for good luck.

grits

Arkansas serves up **traditional** Southern food. Fried chicken, eggplant casserole, and fried green tomatoes are common dishes. The state's many rivers and lakes make it easy to catch and cook catfish, trout, and bass. Barbecue is also popular with Arkansans.

Grits are sometimes enjoyed at breakfast. This is a corn **porridge** that can be served with butter, syrup, or gravy. Collard greens are a vegetable like spinach. They are cooked with ham and onions to create a typical Southern dish. Sometimes Arkansans make wilted lettuce salads. Bacon grease and vinegar are poured over fresh lettuce and radishes or onions.

Festivals

Arkansas holds many fun and quirky festivals each year.
The city of Alma is the Spinach Capital of the World.
People gather there in April for the Alma Spinach Festival.
They enjoy spinach-eating contests and other festivities.
Every May, children can race armadillos at the
World Famous Armadillo Festival in Hamburg.

Arkansas State Fair

fun fact

A statue of Popeye stands in Alma. This cartoon character is known for his love of spinach.

The Bradley County Pink Tomato Festival celebrates the tomatoes grown in the county. The festival has been held every June since 1956. In Little Rock, Riverfest is held beside the Arkansas River on Memorial Day weekend. It is the largest music festival in the state. The capital also hosts the Arkansas State Fair every October.

Folk music is a traditional type of music that often features the fiddle and banjo. Arkansans wrote folk songs about Civil War battles, **outlaws**, and other themes of the South. Folk music is most often heard in the countryside. It is especially popular in the Ozarks.

Mountain View is called the Folk Music Capital of the World. Here, the Ozark Folk Center works to share Arkansas' folk culture. Folk musicians perform there. They also gather in Mountain View's town square to play together. The popularity of folk music in Arkansas represents the state's love for its rich culture and traditions.

Did you know?

One of Arkansas' state songs is a folk tune called "The Arkansas Traveler." It is based on a folktale about a traveler wandering through Arkansas and playing a fiddle.

Fast Facts About Arkansas

Arkansas' Flag

The Arkansas flag has a diamond on a red background. The 25 stars in the diamond's border show that Arkansas was the twenty-fifth state. Three stars inside the diamond represent France, Spain, and the United States. They are the three countries that have controlled Arkansas. A fourth star represents the Confederacy.

State Flower
apple blossom

State Nickname:	The Natural State
State Motto:	*Regnat Populus;* "The People Rule"
Year of Statehood:	1836
Capital City:	Little Rock
Other Major Cities:	Fort Smith, Fayetteville, Springdale
Population:	2,915,918 (2010)
Area:	53,179 square miles (137,733 square kilometers); Arkansas is the 29th largest state.
Major Industries:	farming, services, mining
Natural Resources:	diamonds, coal, bauxite, natural gas, oil, lumber
State Government:	100 representatives; 35 senators
Federal Government:	4 representatives; 2 senators
Electoral Votes:	6

State Bird
mockingbird

State Animal
white-tailed deer

Glossary

bayous—small, slow-moving streams that connect to other bodies of water

Civil War—a war between the northern (Union) and southern (Confederate) states between 1861 and 1865

Confederacy—the group of southern states that wanted to form a new country in the early 1860s; they fought against the northern states during the Civil War.

delta—the area around the mouth of a river

folk—relating to stories, customs, or practices that have been handed down from one generation to the next

gulf—part of an ocean or sea that extends into land

integrate—to bring people of different backgrounds together

Louisiana Purchase—a deal made between France and the United States; it gave the United States 828,000 square miles (2,144,510 square kilometers) of land west of the Mississippi River.

migration—the act of traveling from one place to another, often with the seasons

minerals—natural substances found in the earth

native—originally from a specific place

outlaws—people who are wanted for breaking the law

plains—large areas of flat land

porridge—a food made from boiling grains in milk or water

rodeos—events where people compete at tasks such as bull riding and calf roping; cowboys once completed these tasks as part of their daily work.

service jobs—jobs that perform tasks for people or businesses

springs—areas where water flows up through cracks in the earth

tourists—people who travel to visit another place

traditional—relating to a custom, idea, or belief handed down from one generation to the next

Union—the northern states that remained part of the United States in the early 1860s; they fought against the southern states during the Civil War.

To Learn More

AT THE LIBRARY

Dunn, Joeming W. *Bill Clinton: 42nd U.S. President*. Edina, Minn.: Magic Wagon, 2012.

Lucas, Eileen. *The Little Rock Nine Stand Up for Their Rights*. Minneapolis, Minn.: Millbrook Press, 2011.

Smith, Rich. *Arkansas*. Edina, Minn.: ABDO Publishing, 2009.

ON THE WEB

Learning more about Arkansas is as easy as 1, 2, 3.

1. Go to www.factsurfer.com.

2. Enter "Arkansas" into the search box.

3. Click the "Surf" button and you will see a list of related Web sites.

With factsurfer.com, finding more information is just a click away.

Index

The images in this book are reproduced through the courtesy of: Brandon Alms, front cover (bottom), pp. 8-9; (Collection)/ Prints & Photographs Division/ Library of Congress, pp. 6, 7 (left); Everett Collection/ Newscom, pp. 7 (middle), 17; Bob McNeely/ The White House/ Wikipedia, p. 7 (right); Mark Rightmire KRT/ Newscom, p. 10; Warren Price, pp. 10-11; Robert Franz/ Kimball Stock, pp. 12-13; Gracious_tiger, p. 13 (top); IbajaUsap, p. 13 (middle); Critterbiz, p. 13 (bottom); David R. Frazier Photolibrary, Inc./ Alamy, p. 14 (bottom); Ian Dagnall/ Age Fotostock/ SuperStock, pp. 14-15; Age Fotostock/ SuperStock, pp. 16-17; AgStock Images, Inc./ Alamy, p. 18; Jeff Greenberg/ Age Fotostock, p. 19; Jeff Greenberg/ Alamy, pp. 20-21; Associated Press, p. 21; Mona Makela, p. 22; Matthew Boyer/ Getty Images, p. 23 (top); Jaimie Duplass, p. 23 (bottom); Bryan Thornhill, pp. 24-25; Don Smetzer/ Alamy, p. 26; Pukach, p. 28 (bottom); Pakmor, p. 28 (top); Arto Hakola, p. 29 (left); James Pierce, p. 29 (right).